How to Find What's Missing

with

Archangel Chamuel

There's nothing lost in the Kingdom

Copyright © 2018 Z.Z. Rae

All rights reserved. This book contains material protected under International and Federal Copyright Laws and Treaties. Any unauthorized reprint or use of this material is prohibited. No part of this book may be reproduced or transmitted in any form or by any means, electronic or mechanical, including photocopying, recording, or by any information storage and retrieval system without express written permission from the author/publisher

Café House Publishing *Interlochen/Michigan*

How to Find What's Missing with Archangel Chamuel

There's nothing lost in the Kingdom

Z.Z. Rae

Other Books by Z.Z. Rae

- Your Voice Your Choice: The Value of Every Woman
- Ties of the Heart: How to recover from Divorce and Breakups (A 12 step-by-step healing process)
- I Want to be a Unicorn (Why Unicorns are Real and You can be One

Angel Guidance Series

- Angel Guidance for Wealth (Abundant Living for Everyone)
- Angel Guidance for Dreams (Your Dreams explained by the Angels)
- Angel Guidance for Inner Healing (Heal your Heart, Soul, and Mind with the Angels)
- Angel Guidance for Creativity (Unlock Your Gift)
- Angel Guidance for Peace (Allow life's burdens to fade)
- Angel Guidance for Joy (Raise your Vibrations)
- Angel Guidance for Energy Healing (Aligning your beliefs with your desires)
- Angel Guidance for Awakening Spiritual Gifts (Uncover your natural ability)

Spiritual Tools

- How to Work with Archangels: (Guidance from archangels for abundance, healing, spiritual wisdom, and more.)

- How to Declutter with Archangel Jophiel (How to relieve stress, anxiety, and clutter from your life)
- How to Work with Archangel Michael (How do I know my life's purpose?)

Magical Mermaid Messages

- Magical Mermaid Messages on Abundance (How to manifest money with the law of abundance)
- How to Manifest a Soulmate (with a little help from the mermaids)
- How to Manifest a Soulmate Journal (A journal to attract your soulmate)

Writing Program

- How to Write a Book in 12 Easy Steps
- How to Write a Book in 12 Easy Steps Workbook

Books by Natasha House

Grace Alive Series

Christian Romance

- Grace Alive
- Grace Unbroken

Rebirth of the Prophesy Series

Sci-fi Romance

- Fatal Alien Affection

- Fatal Alien Attraction

The Jade Series

Epic Fantasy

- The Vullens' Curse
- The Deities' Touch
- The Vision Stone

Super Hero Princess Series

Middle grade/Young Adult

- Zara

Non-Fiction

- How to KEEP Writing Your Book
- Illustrated Sermons for Youth or Adults
- Grace Speaks

For all my spiritual friends

Intro

Before I dive into Archangel Chamuel's messages, I wanted to give you a few quick stories about lost items. When I was a little girl, maybe around six, I lost some dimes.

At that age, this was a big deal to me. I used to collect change from the couch or find pennies in odd places. I prayed and asked God where they were.

I soon heard, *"They're downstairs on the living room floor."*

Immediately after, I heard, *"No, they're not."* Then this funny conversation kept happening.

I heard again, *"Yes, they are."*

"No, they're not."

"Yes, they are."

"No, they're not."

"YES, THEY ARE!" The final one shouted it firmly. I ran downstairs, and sure enough, there were my dimes. I never ever forgot that, because that was the first time I remember hearing God or angels.

When I was a teenager, around 17 or so, my only pair of keys to my car got lost. I wasn't driving yet, but I'd already bought my car. We looked everywhere for the keys. I don't know how many months passed by, when my mom heard, *"Why don't you demand those keys to come back."*

As you can see, Mom and I share a similar gift of clairaudience. My mom followed the instructions and commanded the keys to come back. She walked out into the kitchen and sitting on the counter were my keys. She still reminds me of this story, even though I'd actually forgotten about it.

My mom has a phrase, and I felt this book needed it.

There's Nothing Lost in the Kingdom

Let's dive into the messages from Archangel Chamuel. He is known as the angel who helps us find missing items. Although, he is known for more than that, I felt led to open up about this subject. Ready?

Note from the Author

I write what I hear from the divine. Whether it comes from angels, fairies, mermaids, or a divine source. I let their words be authentic. As you dive into this book, have an open mind for the archangels to teach you. Every book I write changes me, and I hope it can bring you healing.

We never worship angels or pray to them, but we can receive help if we are open to it. I believe these angels want to help spread a message of love to everyone who is willing to open their hearts.

-Z.Z. Rae

Chapter 1: Who is Archangel Chamuel?

Inserted from my book: How to Work with Archangels

Archangel Chamuel's name means:

He who sees God.

I always feel warm and fuzzy when I think of Archangel Chamuel. Most consider Chamuel a he, but I've felt a strong feminine energy that's very comforting.

Out of the seven archangels, which is in the 5th century Pseudo-Dionysian teachings, Chamuel is part of the team. Apparently, people sometimes mix Samael, a dark energy who is destructive, with Chamuel. It could be the similarities of their names. Needless to say, Chamuel is definitely an angel of light.

Located in the ancient text, the Kabbalah, Chamuel (as Kamael) is the archangel of the Geburah, the fifth Sephirah (aspect of God) on the Tree of Life. He represents courage and strength through hard times.

Kabbalists contemplate Chamuel (Kamael) as being a part of the Seraphim, which is the peak level of the heavenly angel choir. Because his name means, he who sees God, Chamuel has vision that can see everything.

Archangel Chamuel's Gifts

Self-Love

If you've been having issues of self-hatred or always putting others ahead of yourself, call on Archangel Chamuel to help you balance your self-love. This beautiful angel will help remind you that you're adored and to work on some self-love expressions.

Peace and Divine Justice

Chamuel sticks up for those who are innocent. He pours in his divine strength to help us have the power we need. He helps aid hairdressers, surgeons, air traffic controllers, animal conservationists, and anyone involved in helping keep peace.

Inner Peace

Archangel Chamuel's goal is for global peace, so he helps individuals find their inner peace for their lives when they are going through rocky times.

Missing Items

Chamuel's excellent vision helps you find items you've lost. From his high-altitude view, Chamuel spots our missing items and can clearly see the answers we are looking for with our daily problems. Even though, like a great eagle, Chamuel is at a high level, he still brings himself to our Earthly realm and remains loveable and humble.

Life Purpose

Archangel Chamuel helps guide you toward your life's purpose, a more fulfilling job, a good relationship, home, or anything that you desire—as long as it's for your highest good and aligns with your higher self's purpose.

Colors:

Ruby Red or Pale Green

Crystals and Gemstones:

Red Jasper, Bloodstone, Fluorite, Carnelian, and Pink Tourmaline.

Scents:

Mint, Geranium, Neroli, and Ginger

Zodiac Sign:

Taurus

Archangel Chamuel in a Nutshell

- Self-love
- Peace and Divine Justice
- Inner Peace
- Missing Items
- Life's Purpose, Relationships, Jobs

Message from Archangel Chamuel

I'm here to heighten your awareness of who you truly are. I'm here to pour out loving energy into your heart, soul, and mind, and to help aid the world in abundance of love, joy, and peace. I'm here to provide a path for you, when it seems the path is full of fear. Take my hand, little ones, and I'll guide you around the pitfalls that pop up along the way.

You have a divine purpose, and sometimes it can feel cloudy to see the truest and best path. I'm here to take a fan and blow away all the confusion you've felt in the past. Don't fret about tomorrow, for I'm with you to help you deal with each day.

Forgive daily, and let love flood you concerning your relationships, jobs, and all your accomplishments. You are very beautiful, little ones, and I want to show you that inner beauty always.

Affirmation to Archangel Chamuel

"Dear Archangel Chamuel, thank you for helping me find things that I'm looking for. I gladly ask for help from you concerning my life's purpose, and I thank you for helping me uncover it every day."

Chapter 2: The Missing Piece

Ah, I am so excited to work with you today! I guess you could call me the angel of fun or work, whatever you prefer. I like to enjoy working on things with others. If you step into the mood of, *ugh, I have to find this stupid thing*—we don't get much accomplished.

Often when that last piece is missing, it causes a lot of issues. It may drive you bananas. Have you ever finished a puzzle, only to discover the last piece is nowhere to be found? That feeling. You understand what I'm saying. I'm here to help you find that missing piece, but it's not just about that little piece of cardboard to fit into your perfect picture.

It's much, much more than that, dears. Do you mind if I call you dears? The missing piece, more than anything, is a portion of your life that you feel is *absent*. No one likes that emotion. Like Z.Z. quoted, *there is nothing lost in the Kingdom.*

What is the Kingdom? The Kingdom is righteousness, peace, and joy. So, if you're not feeling those three things, it's time to step back into them. For example, you know that you are your mother and father's child, correct?

You don't question it ever. You may have a different type of family, but you deeply know you were born of specific people, even if they're not what you'd call family.

It's a part of your DNA or heritage. This is a lot how the missing piece goes. It isn't apart from you. I know this sounds woo-woo crazy, but hang on with me here.

In order to find something, you have to grasp that nothing is missing in the first place. No one is happy something is lost, unless they never wanted it to begin with I suppose.

If you've ever lost a best friend, relationship, or family in general, it is devastating. If you've lost a treasure such as a childhood memento or otherwise, it hurts. It doesn't feel like righteousness, peace, or joy to lose something.

What if for one moment you see that thing as a part of you. That it's never been lost to begin with.

Let's start off with relationships for a moment.

When you're little, you may have a variety of different friends. Depending on your personality will be how many friends that come into your life. If you are one of those *one-on-one* people you probably had about two friends at max. As children, your friends become a part of your identity—just like your parents do.

You don't grasp that you are an individual yet, so you hold your identity in others at certain ages. This is why many people gather childhood wounds and have a hard time letting them go later in life.

Have you ever thought about a memory, and it brings up pain that feels just as strong as when you were a child? There's a reason for that.

In those early stages, you are developing your character. It makes me think of someone who is learning their lines in a play. When you are learning your lines, you become the character you are practicing. You take on the role that someone gives you to learn.

This is much how childhood goes. You start off with an innocent mind, and people teach you how to be. They give you a script, and you follow along that script, until you believe that's who you are.

If you were raised in a home that didn't have a good script, you will hold wounds from those moments in your past. What does this have to do with missing things? I'll get to that soon, I promise.

The script tells you what's missing and what's not missing. For example: *I am missing a relationship. I'm single, therefore I am missing out on being married.*

That doesn't feel good to most people. They are told from the time they are little to be in a *couple* is the script. This is why people fall into depression being single. Have you heard the phrase, *my better half?* This phrase breeds into your script that you are a half of a whole person.

Until you let go of that script, you won't be able to receive true joy into your inner being. Your true nature is already whole. Another person doesn't define that. They are simply a reflection of what is already there.

A missing relationship has to turn into the true script which is—I am whole. Once you realize you are whole, you'll find that a healthy person shows up in your life.

Why's that? It's simply because like attracts like. Have you been through relationships that drained you? If you take a hard look at those relationships from the past, what did it teach you? Did you feel like you were missing something, and that person made you feel whole?

Herein lies the problem for most divorces or breakups. They feel that person makes them *complete.* Not that relationships don't make you feel happy or more fulfilled, because they are a reflection of what's going on inside of you.

When you feel like something is missing, it draws another person who feels the same way—if you find any relationship at all.

I want to help you with this situation. If you reach into your script, what is written? Does it say, *without a partner I'm only half here?*

It's time to change that script.

Affirmation

I am a whole person. I look at my script, and I choose what to write.

Chapter 3: Fulfillment

I know I touched on relationships for a minute, and I want to see where that train takes us for a moment longer. Maybe you bought this book to find your missing keys like Z.Z., and I will get to that portion too, but I see the immense struggle people have with the issue of relationships.

Relationships aren't about filling something. It's about receiving what's already filled. If you have a desire for a soulmate, that wish is already fulfilled in the Kingdom.

I'll stick with that phrase, since we started with it. People call it many things: the ether, the energy field, Universe, Kingdom, or a host of other stuff.

When you say a prayer or intention out into the Kingdom, it is already fulfilled right away. When you operate from a sense of fulfillment in yourself, it will shine outward. If you want a relationship, base it from a deep knowing that you already have what you need.

Rewrite your script, dears. Let the words flow out of your heart and find a new way of speaking and believing. Take the pen and paper of your life and write what you want. If you don't take the pen and paper, people will write it for you.

If you don't choose to write your story, your past story will keep writing in automatic mode.

Healing is a huge part of this process, and as you heal, you will uncover that there is nothing missing in your life. The joyfulness of knowing that there is fulfillment inside of you will shine outward in your relationships.

The more you understand the concept of nothing missing and nothing broken in the Kingdom, the more you'll see things being found in your life.

For example: if you feel you are missing a relationship, and you suddenly realize nothing is missing, it will be found. See what I'm saying. The relationship will be hidden from you until you truly believe that nothing is missing inside of you.

A person won't fill your needs. You do. Not that relationships don't aid you, but they are a reflection of something much deeper inside of you. They are your beliefs reflected outwardly around you.

The more you continue to believe that something is missing—the more it will feel like something is missing. No one enjoys the emotions of something lost. Not one person asks for something to be *missing* from their life.

They think that finding someone will bring them peace, love, or fulfillment. Which is not the case. If they find someone, while feeling like a piece is missing, they will only attract more of the missing emotion.

Explore this emotion inside of yourself. Ask, *why do I feel like something is missing from my life? I want to accept that I am whole.*

Once you grasp this, you'll find everything. It'll suddenly show you:

Nothing is Missing

Affirmation

I am whole. Everything I need I receive.

Chapter 4: Where are My Keys?

Every once in a while, you lose something. Everyone does it. I hear about it all the time. *Archangel Chamuel, where are my keys? Where is my wallet? Where is my phone?* There are things that are necessary for your life, and you have to have them. I understand that completely.

Here's a few tips to help you find those things that are missing.

Get Out of Stress Mode

When you step into the fight or flight emotions, it's extremely hard for my voice to get through to you. The first thing to do is *relax.* I know that seems impossible when you have five minutes before you have to leave, and you can't find your keys.

It only takes a moment to breathe. Stress blocks the brain receptors that will give you the answer to your question. Many times, the subconscious goes into lockdown mode when you're freaking out about a missing item. If you take a moment to breathe, relax, and let go, you'll find the answer coming to you extremely quickly.

It can be much like putting a puzzle together. You may receive a little bit at a time, but the whole picture is there. It's not that I don't want to give you the whole picture, but your mind may block the flow of information I am sending your way.

The visual side to finding something can be a challenge for some people, while easy for others. You may need to slow down and tap into your intuitive gift in a very calm manner.

I know this seems impossible when you are stressed about a missing item that is essential for your life.

Let's do a little exercise together.

Step 1

Ask

Ask yourself: *what do I want to find? Do I believe that it's already found?*

Once you acknowledge to yourself that it's actually not lost, but rather your mind has hidden it from you, you can choose to relax your mind. The subconscious actually *knows* where it is, and I work with it in order to help you find whatever you assume is missing.

Once you get into a relaxed mode, and affirm to yourself that it's not lost, but rather hidden at the moment, you can then call it out.

Step 2

Call Your Item Home

Speak directly to the item that it kindly shows itself to you. Once you call it home, trust that it will speak back to you. I know this sounds odd, but everything has a vibration, and if you can pick up on the vibration of the item, you'll find it much quicker.

I will work with you on it.

Step 3

Follow Your Impulses

Many people ignore their first intuitive nudge about where their item is located. Get in tune with those nudges, so that it reveals itself to you.

The more you practice these little steps, the easier it will be to hear, feel, know, or see what you need to do. You'll start to trust your intuition on a deeper level.

You may even get a sense to simply let it go.

Whatever happens, practicing it makes it stronger and stronger. The intuitive side to your nature is like a muscle. When you work it out, it will grow, and be much easier to tap into in the future.

Soon, you'll not only use it for missing items, but everything in general. Remember that everything is energy, and as energy, you can draw it. Speak to yourself phrases like:

- I am a magnet for success.
- I always find what I'm looking for.
- I easily understand my intuition.

- Nothing is missing.
- I ask, and it is given to me.

Affirmation

I open my heart to receive. I ask, believe, and receive.

Chapter 5: Higher Vision

When you're attempting to find something, you often use your Earthly, normal vision. This is why so many of you grow frustrated at the lack of finding something. When you put on what us angels call *higher vision*, you'll start to see things in a whole, new way.

Let me explain to you what that is. Have you ever had a dream that you couldn't quite express, because it was more than images, thoughts, or words? It was hard to put into Earthly terms, because it was a higher vision for your life. The emotion of the dream impacted you, even though you may not know how to put your finger on it.

This is what I want to discuss with you. Higher vision is tapping into the higher-self, your inner being, your soul, or a host of other names you guys have for this part of you. (Laughs) There isn't one right answer when it boils down to the part of you that is divinely connected to God.

When you tap into the God-source within you, you'll start to see everything in a much clearer or higher way. If you're looking for a lost item, ask your inner being, or higher-self to look for you.

Many of you ask me, which is fine, or you ask another energy source to aid you. While we love to help you, sometimes learning this technique for yourself will bring you wonders of self-confidence and joy.

Think of it this way. As children, your parents do a lot for you, but there was something about doing it for yourself that built you up. When you first learned how to tie your shoes, didn't you want to do it by yourself after that? Your parents may have been more efficient at it, but you wanted to learn to do it on your own.

This is what I'm talking about. Although I can use my higher vision to help you right away, I want to build you up, so that you tap into your own higher vision.

Let's try a little exercise to get that higher vision flowing. Ready?

Higher Vision Exercise

Like everything else, this starts with breathing.

- Take a deep breath.

As you connect with your breath, picture the spark of life deep inside of you. Focus in on that spark of love growing and growing through your entire body. As you see it growing, picture that spark turning into a powerful body.

- Step into your inner being's body.

As you step into your inner being's body, focus in on how it feels. Is it warm? Is it vibrant? How do you feel as you connect to the deeper part of you?

- Open your higher vision.

People often call this the third eye, which is a good name for it. For some, the name *third eye* is intimidating, and so I prefer to call it your higher vision.

You have another set of eyes, that isn't limited by Earthly means. It can see beyond.

This is how people see visions of the future, past, or anything spiritual at all.

- Ask to see the truth about what you seek.

When you ask to see the truth, it will reveal itself to you in a variety of ways. Your higher vision will direct you. It may simply be a feeling of *rest*, or it may tell you to *forgive*. There are many things your higher vision could direct you toward.

If someone stole the item from you, you may be asked to simply forgive the thief. When you forgive, it opens new doors for something to be found. Such as: a random gift from someone, it returned to you, a sense of peace, or an expanded mind.

You may see something you've never seen before. Simply ask.

- See it as done.

Here's where many people trip up. Once they ask about the missing item, they struggle with letting it be done. They want to know *how, where, and why.* Often times, the higher part of you will give you simple instructions, which you don't all enjoy.

I am here to assist you with tapping into your higher vision and growing accustomed to using it as often as you need it. You can do this for many things, not just missing items. If you feel anything is lacking in your life, you can do this exercise, and I will be there to help you.

Sometimes you may feel a sense of purposelessness, and I am helpful for that too. A thing doesn't make you purposeful, nor an action. Staying tuned into your source is what helps you remain purposeful.

You and you alone are a purpose. You are here to spread love wherever you go.

Are you ready to tap into your higher vision?

Affirmation

I tune into my higher vision. I open myself up for the answers I seek.

Chapter 6: Being Okay

I know you don't all like to hear this, but can you be okay without that item in your life? Can you keep enjoying what you have, and let go of what has been lost?

For example: if you had a relationship which fell apart, and all you can think of is how to get it back, how will you live your life?

Backwards. Full of regret. Sadness.

None of those emotions are pleasant for you. When you live in a stream of loss, loss will keep showing up in your life. When you let go, be okay, and move forward with whatever it is you felt you lost, you will find a better thing awaiting you.

Sometimes you don't know what was lost—actually needed to be lost. Why do I say that? Because, until something was lost, you may not have realized how *found* it was inside of you. I know this may seem strange but hear me out.

When you lose a relationship, even though it was tragic in the moment, later on, it may have been the best thing for you. You may have uncovered some deep root issues of co-dependency. If you let the loss teach you a lesson, you'll uncover that everything you need is already found.

Every Soul has a Choice of Being Lost or Found

When you feel loss, over and over, you must examine why you feel everyone else is your source of feeling found. The sense of wholeness doesn't come from an outside source, but rather tuning into your true nature, or your higher-self, as some would call it.

When you tune into that part of you, you'll uncover that everything you need is found. I like to keep things on a practical level, so let me dive into some more information about this entire thing.

Think of it this way. When you depend on another person for your found-ness, you will experience loss at one point. When you focus only on them for creating happiness, joy, peace, and love inside, you will feel loss—always.

I'm not trying to put this doom and gloom mentality on you, but when you realize that the source of what you need isn't outside, you'll operate from a place of *found-ness*. It won't feel like anything is missing—ever.

This is what I'm here for. I'm helping you tap into the source of who you truly are, so that you can operate from that place. When something goes missing, and I'm addressing relationships, because this seems to bring you the most pain, I try to help you find the self-love that recovers you from what's missing.

Once you uncover that nothing is missing, because love is inside of you the entire time, you'll operate from that place, and love will flow outward easily.

Needless to say, you will still experience emotions of loss when someone leaves your life, but you can recover much quicker when you understand the principles that I'm relaying to you here.

Human experience always incorporates loss. Once you recognize your dependency on another, you'll uproot that and move forward.

Friends

If you observe the friendships you've had over the years, you'll grasp what I'm talking about. How many people have come and gone in your experience here on Earth? Did you have a BFF as a kid, in school, or as a teenager, and now you have them on social media or never contact at all anymore?

You still functioned with or without them in your life. You moved on. You may have moved on with a lot of pain, but you still understood that you could live without them.

Friends are there for seasons, and some are there to teach you lessons, while others are there to show you different sides to people in general. Not everyone commits to sticking by someone for life. You may see why you attracted the friend you did, because once they left, an emotion sprang up.

The closer you are to a friend, the more you'll grasp what your inner being is trying to teach you. Do you depend on them for connection, understanding, or love? If so, once they leave, you'll feel pain, because your inner being is trying to tell you: *that was not your source. Your source is the opposite of what you feel right now. It is fully committed to you.*

Family

This one is extremely tough for most people. When family comes and goes, it can bring a much deeper sense of something missing. Whether through death or another form of loss, family may bring the greatest feelings of betrayal or sorrow.

Not everyone thinks of the word family the same. You may have a deep commitment to love, protect, and respect your family, but not everyone has that same level of commitment. Family members may leave you with a sense of *not good enough, fear, anxiety, depression, or black sheep* emotions.

If you have a unique set of beliefs, as opposed to your family, understand that it's okay to be in your own set of beliefs. Your family has their individual paths, and so do you. If you can grasp that being *found* in who you are will not only help you, but your family too, you can allow yourself to go into that position.

Why do I say it will help your family too?

When you allow yourself to be in your own power, you inadvertently give your family permission to be in their own power too.

If you rely fully on your family's approval for everything, you'll experience loss.

What kind of loss?

- Loss of personal power
- Loss of personal experiences
- Loss of understanding yourself

If you have experienced death in your family, and you relied on that family member for any of the above: personal power, decision making, experiences, understanding, or love, it will take a bit of time to come back to the connection within yourself.

Learn the Lessons in the Grief

If you're faced with what you wished you would have done or said, grasp the lesson in that. Make it your highest priority to express yourself to those you love.

If you have a hard time letting go of a passed loved one, remember that their energy is still with you by means of your emotions, thoughts, and memories.

When you connect to the good times, you keep that connection alive. When you rely on that connection for your source of love, it will feed loss.

Tune inward to find Source, so that when loss hits you, you can work through it easier.

Affirmation

I connect to myself. I am whole.

Chapter 7: Confirmation

When you are seeking something, confirm to yourself that no matter what, it is found. When you do this, it's like marking a checklist off in spirit. When you do that, the confirmation will show up in a way you need.

Here's a little prayer I'd like to give you to help you with this:

Prayer

Dear God,

I ask for my highest and best to be done in this situation. Thank you, God, for bringing to me clarity that I am fully found in love. Whatever is missing is an outward expression of something I need to connect. I now connect to love inside of me. I am healed, healthy, whole, loved, accepted, and complete. Amen.

Stolen Items

When something has been stolen, and you want it found, it is a whole different type of energy. The emotions involved with something being stolen is anger, unfairness, and a wanting of justice. I completely understand. I want you to know that it *is* an injustice when someone steals something from you.

Here's where I want to help you.

When someone is stealing something from someone else, they are completely powerless. They think by the having of that thing, they will feel better. It is a sense of taking someone else's hard work, energy, or time.

This can manifest in a variety of different ways. This may come not just from stolen items, but from people who steal your time too. You may have a big conversation with someone, only to have them do the opposite of all the wisdom you poured out on them.

This can leave you with the emotion of thievery, because they wasted something precious to you—your time and energy.

Those who want help, yet don't administer it when given it, are not operating from a place of power. If you can grasp this, you can understand how to better protect your time, energy, and items.

Forgiveness

I know, I know, this isn't something you probably want to hear right now. Especially if someone stole something from you. Archangel Michael gave some examples in: *How to Work with Archangel Michael,* but I also want to address this.

When someone violates another (through thievery, energy-sucking, time…) you have a personal choice to make.

Here's a few tips.

Tip 1

Give Them Back Their Power

Archangel Michael addressed this too, but I find it necessary for you to hear again. Those who do any of the above, are powerless people. They don't operate from their soul—they are in lack. When they function from this place of lack, they will attempt to take your power.

When you give them back their power, you go free.

How do you do this?

- Make them responsible for their actions.

Whether you left something out, which may have been a bad choice, give that person's responsibility back to them. Recognize that they are powerless by stealing something from you and give them back their power.

Whether in person or not, say to them: *you are responsible for your poor choices, and I give those choices back to you. I take back my power in this situation.*

- Let go of the anger.

It's completely normal to be angry when someone steals an item from you. They took a part of your energy, and it is an injustice for them to do so. They became a powerless person in that moment, because they didn't function in their own energy but yours.

When you let go of anger and recognize this situation for what it was—powerlessness—you can offer a hand of compassion. Whether that person fesses up, changes or not, you can bring back your personal power by giving them back theirs.

Recognize that they are not in control of their own energy, and as a result they take other people's items.

- The item is not your source.

If you grasp that the item you got stolen is not your source of happiness, it can be much easier to let it go. The person who took it will not be satisfied either. Not really. They may think they got away with something, but their true essence will fight them on it.

When you fully acknowledge that nothing outside of yourself is your source, you'll easily let go, forgive, and move forward in your life. If you're fearful about recovering financially from the situation, tap into the source of where everything comes from.

The money will be there for a new one.

Hold your power in this situation. Pull it back to you. Give back that person their choices, and you'll see things you've never seen before. When you offer compassion back to the person who stole from you, it frees YOU.

Affirmation

I give back others their power. I forgive all those who've stolen from me. I tap into love.

Chapter 8: The Wave of Power

There is a personal power waiting for you. It's always available inside of you. It's a matter of turning on the flow. When you are searching for something in your life, go with the flow to find what it is you need.

Trust the flow of ease, power, and love. When you feel at ease with something, you'll find it showing up in your life in a quicker way.

If you hold angst over something, you will find it avoiding you. Do you ever notice how the more stressed you get about finding something, the more it seems to avoid you? When you take a deep breath, relax, and let go, it shows itself very quickly.

Why is that?

When you offer the flow to your mind, it will open doors for you. The flow is what I call *ease, relaxation, and an offering of peace* to your mind. The mind operates 110% easier when it's in the state of flow.

This is why people get deep revelations during prayer, meditation, or deep breathing exercises. They tap into the flow to uncover what their soul needs in order to move them forward.

Forward motion is inevitable, but if you are paddling up the stream, you will only find yourself growing more and more angsty. Here's a few ways to unlock the flow.

- Give something away.

If you are missing something in your life, tap into the flow, and give something away with great joy. If you feel a lack of money in your life, tap into the joy of giving. When you give, you unlock a lot of different sides to yourself. You understand that there is no missing things in your life, but rather a sense of flow and ease.

- Separate yourself from that which is lost.

When you identify with that which is lost in your life, you will continue to live from that sense of loss. When you grasp that you are not that thing, but rather you are the flow that can lead you to anything, you'll find yourself at ease with life.

You won't stress about the wrongness or rightness to anything, because you'll grasp that the flow is taking you in the right direction.

- Loss will teach you something.

When you let loss teach you a lesson, you'll find your stream moving easier and easier. You'll see it, let go, and move forward with ease. Essentially, you'll grasp that *stuff* isn't the source of love. It's your connection to your true essence—which is love.

What is the Flow?

When you tap into the flow, it's tapping into the highest and best good for your life. When you learn lessons from where the flow takes you, it will free you from the fear of loss. You'll let yourself go down the stream with ease, and if you run into a few rocks, you'll understand them for what they are.

If you identify with the rocks, you'll stay there, but if you remember you're the stream not the rocks, you'll flow around the blockages.

There are great lessons in feeling like something is missing from your life. If you see others getting what you want, you may have several emotions that surface.

- Jealousy
- Guilt
- Fear
- Loss
- Anxiety
- Anger

All of you must learn the lesson of flow. When something shows up in your world, whether it's someone else has what you want, someone stole what was yours, or other ways of loss, you can look at it for what it is.

Things outside of me aren't my source. People outside of me aren't my source. Things and people come and go.

You may have a relationship that you swear would always be there in your life, but one day it's not. Whether from divorce, breakups, or death, that relationship is not your source. If so, you will experience much greater emotion if you attach yourself to the person as your source.

Not that you don't connect in love to others, but when you come from that place of deep connection within, you can freely give without fear. So many people give with fear. They think, *if I just give hard enough they won't leave my life.*

When they operate out of this lack mentality, the other person cannot stay in that stream—it's too uncomfortable. They will feel smothered or a host of other emotions, because they have become a source of love for the other person.

If you're not connected to your source, you'll always feel something missing from your life. Let the flow take you to connection. If the flow is painful, allow it to still take you there. It will. I promise.

Becoming self-aware is healing for everyone.

Affirmation

I become aware of myself. I tap into the flow. I allow myself to go with the flow of life. I trust it will lead me.

Chapter 9: The End Result

The end result to all of this is—get into the flow. When you uncover the reasoning for the sense of loss in your life, you'll soon find yourself reconnecting. When you look at the lost item for what it is—something to learn from—you will find that you recover it quicker.

Have you ever thought, *I always lose the good things in my life?* If you are dwelling on that rock, and you are trying to flow, it won't feel good. You'll keep running into that blockage again and again.

Instead, recognize it for what it is—a rock. When you look at the rock and think, *this isn't me. This rock is showing me something here. Why do I feel this thing is my source of happiness?* Once you identify the rock, it's much easier to flow around it.

Let Go of Resistance So That You Can Flow Forward

People think resistance is bad. Resistance is teaching you something. It's showing you something inside of yourself. When you experience the emotions of loss, ask yourself, *why am I identifying with this thing I lost? What is my true source? Can I flow around this item? Can I recognize this for what it is, and move past it?*

When you move past it, you will find several things happening:

- Better things show up
- You learn a valuable lesson
- You tap into the joy of letting go

- Someone gives you something
- The resources come in

I've seen this happen again and again for people. When you finally go with the flow, everything you desire starts showing up. When you let go of what was lost, suddenly everything you want is found. The more resistance is addressed, the more you see what was missing as part of your life's experience.

When You Let Go of Loss, You Are Found

What if you truly trusted that the things that are missing are lessons for you to look at? Give yourself back your power in these forms of losses. When you do that, you'll see everything with your higher vision.

Affirmation

I let go of resistance. I tap into my true source.

Chapter 10: Creating Something New

In you is millions of creations. Every minute you are creating something new. Your thoughts, emotions, and outward expressions are like mini bursts of energy that create something. When you continue on a stream of thought, you will eventually be led to what your thoughts are building.

Be careful what thoughts you're investing your time, energy, and emotions into. If you find that your thoughts feel out of control about what's lost, take a moment to see from your higher vision. See it for what it is. They are Earthly fears that there isn't enough, or a host of other things that the mind creates.

What is anxiety?

People experience anxiety when they throw themselves into a probable future that won't happen, unless they keep feeding the thought pattern they're currently in. When you pull yourself back into the power of the flow, you'll let go of what could happen tomorrow.

If you have a fear of loss with a relationship, you feed that relationship with the energy of loss, until they may leave you. You've probably seen it over and over.

You want them to *prove you wrong* when it comes to the loss energy, but if you nonstop fed someone a blue popsicle wouldn't their tongue turn blue?

I know that's a funny example, but people may resist what you're saying for a while, but eventually they'll do two things: adapt to your energy or leave your energy. It results in the same thing—a loss.

If someone believes the opposite of what you believe, they will resist your words for a while. You may find someone trying to prove themselves to you or vice versa, until one of the energies wins out. Then energy will shift in some way.

Either you deal with your fears, or they will continue to show you something.

In the loss, there is a revelation about your energy. If you examine the fear of loss, you'll uncover a root belief you can work on healing and letting go of.

If you choose to live in loss, you will attract those who will show you that belief system in several ways:

- They themselves have great fear too
- They want to change you, but their own energy runs out

- They reflect your fear

Any one of these will be feeding the wrong kind of flow. Once you can recognize fear of loss, you'll be able to step out of that flow and into a new one. You'll suddenly find yourself attracting the right kind of relationship, because fear is no longer blocking the flow.

Your Beliefs Will Be Reflected Wherever You Are

If you find yourself losing jobs, relationships, items, or anything like that, it's time to examine a few internal blocks.

Where is the belief coming from? Is it coming from fear or love? Are you showing yourself the same compassion, understanding, and love that you want from others?

When you tap into your internal flow of wholeness, you'll see others in your realm with a much clearer picture. No longer will you try to get them to prove themselves to you or vice versa, you'll simply dwell in your flow, and allow them the same privilege.

Affirmation

I tap into wholeness. I step into the present moment. I learn lessons I need to learn.

Chapter 11: Creating the Flow

Creating is in your power at all times. Every second of every day you are in creative mode, because you are a natural creator by design. You come from the great creator, who gave you the same abilities in your day-to-day life.

When you think a thought, see it as a little ball of energy. The more thoughts you think around a subject, the more that energy grows with power. Eventually, that energy will move into action, and soon the action will show up into the physical realm.

When you see loss wherever you go, you'll only feed the energy of loss in your life. You won't feel satisfied with the flow, because the flow isn't pleasant. When you let go of the fear of loss, and let it teach you something, you'll soon uncover a brand-new creative power.

The Power to Overcome Fear

Whenever loss is involved, there is fear involved. When you go beyond the fear, you'll let things take you forward. Whether it was a loss of a job, friendship, relationship, or precious item, you'll see that you keep moving past these things—one way or another. If you see them repeating in a cycle, grab ahold of the lessons.

Why do these people, jobs, or things hold all your power?

Once you see that they are reflections of something, you can reclaim what was lost. After learning the lesson, you'll go with the stream, and it will take you to a place of extreme power again.

You'll see that love is power. When you show love to the shadow parts of yourself—the parts that reflect something greater—you'll be able to understand that these parts aren't supposed to be abhorred, but rather adored.

When You Adore the Lessons in the Loss, You'll be Freed Again and Again

You'll find yourself detaching from things, people, and memories. It'll be easier and easier to let go and go with the flow of life. You'll see it for what it is—a lesson to be learned, and move past it.

Learning to Flow is Essential to Life

When you hold onto loss, it can't actually teach you what you need to know. When you're in a relationship, and someone is leaning on you for emotional power, you offer your support, but you don't accept their power as your own. I hope that makes sense.

You Can't Fix Someone Else's Problem

They must tap into their own source, and let the flow take them to the solution. If you offer your hand, and they refuse to take it, you don't have to worry about them anymore. They have been offered another solution, even if they are refusing each and every solution to their problem.

Their stream will take them to where they need to go. They must learn their own lessons in life. When you recognize this, even if it caused you pain or loss, it can bring healing in that area.

Every One of You has Creative Power

Every one of you has a stream of love to take you to your solution. You may be a part of someone else's solution for a while, but they must still choose to look at that in themselves. Once they do, they must take their power back.

If they give their power away again and again, there isn't much you can do about it. You must trust their stream to take them to their solution.

When you recognize a relationship as a lesson, it can free you to move forward in personal power. When experiencing great loss, there is a time of letting go, forgiving, and moving past the lesson. It's not always an instant thing to learn something.

Think about school. When you go to school, you study, you grow, and you learn over a period of time. You don't instantly know everything about a subject. This is how life lessons can appear too.

- You may have had similar experiences of loss, but what have each one of them taught you?
- Did you refuse to see the lesson in it?
- Was the lesson too hard to look at?

If so, you'll repeat it, until your heart connects back to its true source. Once you do, you'll find yourself moving forward again.

Let life teach you what you need to know. Flow with the stream.

Affirmation

I flow with the stream to learn what I need to know. I let people learn their lessons too. I forgive easily.

Chapter 12: Welcome Change

Not many people like change. Change can bring loss, but in that change, can you see how it helped you in some way? Learning the lessons, in the loss, will bring great healing and revelation.

I know I keep addressing relationships, and this is because I can feel how deeply wounded some of you are as you read my words. It's not just about finding your iPod, or a random thing you lost 15 years ago, but finding a sense of identity in yourself. When you identify with the loss, and make it who you are, you'll find yourself getting stuck in the past.

For example: if you lost a marriage, and you label yourself as divorced, you will identify with that situation again and again. If you simply see yourself as learning lessons through relationships, it will free you to give yourself back your power.

If you feel innocence is lost, and you want to reclaim that, go to the place in your heart where there is a connection to innocence. Before someone left were you a different person? Learn the lesson in that loss and let yourself feel innocence again.

If you give that person your innocence, you are letting them take your sense of self and power. When you realize innocence is not a moment, but who you are, you will pull back that emotion to yourself.

You can go back to the innocence you enjoy, and let it take you to where you need to forgive, let go, and heal.

Can Your Lessons Help Others Heal?

This is a big one. When you look at things you've lost, can you turn it into a lesson to help others heal? When you heal portions of loss in your heart, you'll start to recognize when someone else is in a similar situation. This gives you ample opportunity to reach out a hand to them. Of course, they must take the advice and flow with it.

It's never your fault if you try to help, and someone rejects that help. It's not you they're rejecting, it's their lack of power inside themselves. If you are trying to get someone to connect to their lessons, you may experience some heartache.

If you are a teacher, you can understand that you can give people all the resources in the world, but if your student doesn't apply those resources, it's not your fault. The greatest teachers on the planet still have to be received.

Go with the flow and follow where you feel led to speak up.

Affirmation

I welcome change in my life. I let my lessons lead me forward.

Chapter 13: Sending Out Angels

To give you a clear picture, I want to talk a bit more about recovering a missing item. I want to discuss when something physical is missing such as:

- Keys
- Wallet
- Phone
- Precious jewelry

There are a few things I can advise you on. You have a host of angels willing and able to help you at all times. If you give them permission to seek out the item you have lost (misplaced is a better word), they will go on an assignment to hunt down that item for you.

As in Z.Z.'s story, her keys were retrieved and brought back from their misplaced spot. This can be the case for you too. When you speak to the host of angels, who are excellent at finding things, they will start their search for you. This can come in a variety of ways.

- The item suddenly appears
- You get an impulse to look in an odd spot or the same spot you've already looked
- You replace the item, and it shows up
- You forgive someone, and a blessing comes to you

I lovingly call these angels 'detective angels', because they search out an uncover the mystery of the lost item. If it is something you can't replace such as precious jewelry, ask for clear, concise instructions from these angels. They are my helpers in the task of uncovering misplaced items.

Sometimes these angels are in the form of people. You may hear someone say, *have you checked the side of your bed?* Maybe you did, but when they said that, you felt the need to do it again, and suddenly there it was.

Saying a Prayer of Protection

If it feels like things keep going missing, speak a prayer of protection over your personal belongings. I myself or Archangel Michael will step in and clear the energy around your home. Sometimes things going missing is a sign of low-energy hanging around. This low energy can be a form of belief in yourself, or something you need to clear in your home.

Smudge

Sometimes it's best to do a simple routine of smudging your home of lower energy. When you do a smudging, whether through prayer, sage, or another form, it can help your mind clear up, so that you can connect to your higher vision.

Let Go of the Need to be in Control of the Outcome

When you do this, you give us angels permission to find your missing item, even when it doesn't make logical sense. Such as the case of Z.Z.'s keys—them suddenly appearing on the counter didn't make logical sense.

If you think your item will only be found through logic, or where you remember last putting that item, it'll limit the results for you. Instead, let go of the need to control where and how the item returns to you.

If you've studied the law of attraction, you understand the laws of the universe quite well. When you ask, it is already given, and it is your job to get into the flow, so that ease will take you to your answer.

Ease and flow are key.

Affirmation

I let go of control. I flow. I call on my detective angels to find my misplaced items.

Chapter 14: Rewriting the Old Story

Sometimes when I look at someone, I will see strings—like taffy all around them. This is built up energy from the past. Many of you tell the same story again and again about what's missing in your life. This book isn't just to find your keys, wallet, or phone, but dealing with loss in general.

How many times have you talked about what's missing from your life?

For example:

I don't have enough money.

I can't afford what I want.

I hate my job. I want something better.

I'm single, and I only attract losers.

I want to be happy.

I don't know where this item is.

I can't find purpose in my life.

On and on, and I could write a slew of other stories. It's not the wallet or phone that really bothers you—it's the deeper things you crave. Connection. Love. Freedom. These are the things your heart is reaching out for. Many times, it's afraid to take the drastic inner shifts it needs to get to the new story.

Start off a little at a time. That's what I always instruct people to do. Let's do a little exercise today.

Exercise

- What is the story I tell myself every day?

First, identify what it is you're repeating, or it can be hard to really pinpoint it. Many times, these are thoughts that you are unaware of that loop.

I hate being single. Why can't I find my soulmate? I wanted to be married so much younger. I want kids, and I can't find a partner.

How many times do you repeat something like this in your mind? Do you rehash the disappointments from all the previous relationships or situations that have led you to those conclusions? Do you go through statistics in your head about other relationships you observe?

I might as well give up on love. No one will want me. I try so hard, and no one is attracted to me. Maybe I'm ugly…

I'm sorry for writing such a negative paragraph in here, but can you recognize some of these thoughts rolling around inside of your mind? They can be subtle, and if left unattended, they will build up an emotion that can be overwhelming.

Loss.

When you feel something is missing, it will drudge up the emotions of loss. You will remember every instance where someone hurt you, left you, or passed away. You will compare those situations with the current thoughts, and it will build up a stream of negative emotion that can leave you crippled.

If you're facing the same situation with a different face, it's time to look inward. This isn't an outside problem, but a belief situation.

This is how many face depression. They drag not only the present situation in their mind, but the past ones too. Think of the momentum that causes in the body, mind, and heart.

- Change the story

I know that sounds easy, but think of something you've memorized again and again. Now, try to look at something else and memorize that instead. You more in likely have the first script rolling around in your mind for a little while.

When a thought comes up such as: *I'll never find someone.*

Replace it with a new story like: *so and so found a mate, and there has to be someone for me too.*

Maybe it's not super positive yet, but it's a start in the right direction. Start where you are and begin to rewrite the mental story you tell yourself every day.

- Practice, practice, practice

Like everything in life, you have to practice to make perfect. When your old stories pop up, it will take practice to put your mind back on the right path. If loss arises, or old emotions, tell yourself a better-feeling story.

Once you do, you'll start seeing how to improve every day.

Affirmation

I tell myself a better story today. I let go of the old stories.

Chapter 15: Repetition

As children, you learn by repeating again and again. This form of learning is how the subconscious operates. When you feel something is missing, you have to tell that part of yourself a new story.

I have everything I need.

I am complete.

Whenever I ask, it is given.

I am right on time.

When you start by repeating a better story to yourself, you'll find things aligning with those statements very quickly. You can call on me to help you with finding what's missing, and I will assist you.

Missing items can be many things, and sometimes people don't realize I will help with everything they feel is missing.

- Relationships
- Jobs
- Life purpose
- Self-love
- Peace
- Joy
- Hope
- Restoration
- Items
- Precious memories

If you need help with any feelings of loss, come to me, and I will help you immediately. There is a process to healing from loss or an old story you've told yourself for a long time.

This is a big one for people:

I wasted so much time.

It's too late for me.

I'm too old.

I can't tell you how many times I hear that story. You humans think in such linear time. Some of you may not marry until you're 40+ but think of it this way. If you marry when you're older, what kind of wisdom will you carry into a relationship? If you've learned lessons from everything you've faced, and apply it now, you will have a fantastic relationship.

If you are wanting children, there are so many options for you. Age is a number; it's not a death sentence to your dreams. There are countless women who have children in their elder years, or there is the option of adoption.

Many people start off at an older age following their dreams, because they finally wake up to what they truly want. They may face feelings of regret, but the ones who channel those lessons are the ones who succeed.

Repeat What You Want

The energy of what you want is already there. It's a matter of tuning into it or getting into alignment with those things. You've probably heard that before, right? (Laughs)

Your subconscious mind will avoid what you're not ready for. If you have on repeat what you don't want, it only brings you more of that—because that's what it does.

If you start speaking a new story, your subconscious starts turning toward that new story. It's like coaxing an animal with some food. A little at a time it comes toward you, until it trusts you again.

You can't just throw the food in its face and expect it to believe you right away. You have to train your brain to think in terms of *possibilities*.

Affirmation

I am ready to repeat a new story. Everything I desire is possible.

Chapter 16: Keep it Simple

Sometimes people complicate everything when it comes to finding what's missing. It becomes more about trying to fill something, rather than understanding there is no lack, and operating from that emotional space.

Many of you, if not all, have been trained in the area of lack. It is human nature to look for what is lacking, instead of what is fulfilled in your life. The more you focus on the *lost* things in your life, the more those items elude you in many ways.

Taking the time to breathe in wholeness every day, will help your mind, body, soul, and spirit remember that it is already full. When you operate from that place of fullness, you'll find your desires showing up in meaningful ways.

You won't even barely *ask*, and it will show up. Such as:

It would be nice to share my love with someone.

I love feeling whole, and I love giving to others.

I want to help people connect to themselves.

There are many ways you may share the wholeness you feel. There is always something you'll be wanting, but the wanting can feel delicious, rather than sorrowful. When you know every time you ask, it is given energetically, you can rest in that knowledge deep inside.

Practice every day connecting to the depth of wholeness inside of you. Show up for yourself in meaningful ways every day, and you'll see what's missing becoming clearer and clearer.

When something is missing—it is simply a reflection of what you assume is missing on the inside too.

How many have you thought:

I always lose everything!

I'm so annoying, why don't I put things back where they belong?

I've always been dumped, I'm going to get dumped again.

I hate losing things.

Why do I always do this?

Why don't people stay?

Why do I lose money?

Get my drift? There are streams of thoughts that support what you are missing. When you replace that stream of thought with a new thought or emotion, you will find what you are supposedly missing.

If you operate from the place of wholeness, things that you don't have won't seem as important, and you'll stop focusing on the lack of it. Once you do, your original *asking* will finally start moving toward you, because now there is no resistance in that area.

Picture every time you ask, there is an immediate stream that will carry you toward what you are wanting. If you put a boulder in the way, which is a thought of resistance, then it will take you much longer to get you to where you need to go.

Trust the Stream to Take You There.

Affirmation

When I ask, it is given.

Chapter 17: I am Found

Anytime something is found there is a sense of relief. You feel better, because the item that caused you stress is now back in your hands. It becomes tangible to you. Such as:

- An item
- Relationship
- Spiritual connection
- Job
- Money

What if you could flow in the stream of it being found, before it physically manifests itself in the natural world? Wouldn't that also feel like relief?

Here is where I want to take you for a moment.

When you ask, immediately tap into the sense of relief of having that what you asked for. Don't second guess it, simply rest in the having of it, and let the stream open you up to take you there.

- Where do you feel led to go?
- What connections do you feel you need to make?
- Are emotions coming up to release?

All of this is good. When you learn to recognize the feelings of the stream (or relief) you will find it easier and easier to tap into that flow.

Believe in divine timing, and that timing will show up. So many people think that things are random. While, yes, some situations may be unpredictable in life, many times it's the blockage of the flow which is creating the events you see in the physical realm.

If you are not getting what you want, there is a boulder in the way that you are focusing on. If you simply let go of the boulder, you will naturally flow around it. This may be seasons of letting go emotionally, challenging yourself, or growing in some way, but those impulses will take you further.

Let the Stream Take You There

If you're wondering what the stream is, here is the best way to explain it. The stream is your natural state of ease. The stream is the source which leads you to your desires.

Breaking it down into a simple term I'd call it this—Source. There are many different names for the source of energy which flows through you and to you. If you tap into the essence of relief, flow, love, and joy, Source is always there for you.

When you resist the natural source inside of you, it will cause discomfort or pain. This is because your true self is wishing you to connect with your ultimate source.

The desires will always be formulating, and source responds to them. Your stream fluxes as your desires flux. If you feel like you used to want one thing, but you've changed your mind, that's okay. Source knows that, and it will ultimately shift with your desires.

The key is to relax. The more you go with the stream, or Source within you, you'll find things naturally showing up in your life. You'll get impulses, ideas, or relationships that support your asking.

Affirmation

I let the stream of my desire take me where I need to go.

Chapter 18: Loss and Letting Go

If you've lost a relationship, I want to help you for a moment with this. There are many ways to look at this loss. Some people come into your life as a result of your asking, but they also have a personal stream or source too. If they are in resistance to their stream, they may cause unneeded pain in both of you.

Every one of you has a personal choice to let go of control and go with the flow. If you feel a need to control someone's behavior, you will find yourself feeling disconnected from Source.

Source Doesn't Control—it Flows Freely

If you feel you need to hang onto a relationship, I want to help you shift that. A relationship should have ease and flow. It should feel natural to connect and come together with someone. If there is much resistance, you must ask yourself a few things.

- *Why do I want something difficult?*
- *Am I feeling loss, and I think they are the cure?*
- *Am I trying to control the outcome?*
- *Am I giving them free choice, and making them responsible for their actions?*
- *Can I recognize my blocks, and trust the flow?*

Not that there isn't bumps in a relationship, but a healthy relationship should feel at ease and flow. You will run into resistance within each other, but that's where you can recognize it for what it is, and let it go. Whether it's letting go of your own resistance, or letting them figure out their source of resistance, it can bring peace to you.

If you feel this one person is the source of your happiness, there will be resistance in that thinking. You will find that person going against that stream, because that's not who they are. They must be in their own power, and you in yours for it to work correctly.

Relationships that Echo

Relationships echo something. They always do. If you want someone back in your life, yet they resist you, it's time to look at the echo in yourself.

- *Why do you want someone who doesn't want you?*
- *Are you basing your self-worth on their resistance of you?*

It's time to step back into ease and flow. If that relationship is nothing but rocks, can you make a healthy choice to let it go? It doesn't mean it will permanently end forever, but until that partner can align with you, there will be pain.

Your Self-worth is Not Based on Another

This is a powerful lesson for each and every one of you. In society, it is often taught that having a partner is your sense of worth. If someone loves you—you're worthy.

This is straight up bullshit. Excuse me for swearing, but it is. Your self-worth is not based on another's resistance. If they are constantly battling you for a sense of power, you will find yourself miserable.

They must be in their own power, and you must be in yours.

If not, you will find a lot of issues popping up left and right. This is why *drama queens* find one another in a relationship. They both have issues that need flow and healing, and they will echo them back and forth in themselves.

Affirmation

I let go of that which no longer serves me.

Thank you for reading:

How to Find What's Missing with Archangel Chamuel

Visit: eepurl.com/cV-Trf for your

FREE

GIFT

Angel Guidance for Wealth

If you've enjoyed this book, I would love for you to post a review. As an author, I am always learning and growing, and I'd love to hear back from you.

Come visit me on:

Facebook: Z.Z.'s Angel Card Corner

Instagram: @Z.Z.Rae

Blog: www.angelguidancetoday.wordpress.com

Facebook Group: Angel Guidance, Fairies, Mermaids, and Unicorns Magical Realm

Website: https://authorzzrae.wixsite.com/zzrae

YouTube: ZZ Rae ASMR

Other Books by Z.Z. Rae

- Your Voice Your Choice: The Value of Every Woman
- Ties of the Heart: How to recover from Divorce and Breakups (A 12 step-by-step healing process)
- I Want to be a Unicorn (Why Unicorns are Real and You can be One

Angel Guidance Series

- Angel Guidance for Wealth (Abundant Living for Everyone)
- Angel Guidance for Dreams (Your Dreams explained by the Angels)
- Angel Guidance for Inner Healing (Heal your Heart, Soul, and Mind with the Angels)
- Angel Guidance for Creativity (Unlock Your Gift)
- Angel Guidance for Peace (Allow life's burdens to fade)
- Angel Guidance for Joy (Raise your Vibrations)
- Angel Guidance for Energy Healing (Aligning your beliefs with your desires)
- Angel Guidance for Awakening Spiritual Gifts (Uncover your natural ability)

Spiritual Tools

- How to Work with Archangels: (Guidance from archangels for abundance, healing, spiritual wisdom, and more.)

- How to Declutter with Archangel Jophiel (How to relieve stress, anxiety, and clutter from your life)
- How to Work with Archangel Michael (How do I know my life's purpose?)

Magical Mermaid Messages

- Magical Mermaid Messages on Abundance (How to manifest money with the law of abundance)
- How to Manifest a Soulmate (with a little help from the mermaids)
- How to Manifest a Soulmate Journal (A journal to attract your soulmate)

Writing Program

- How to Write a Book in 12 Easy Steps
- How to Write a Book in 12 Easy Steps Workbook

Books by Natasha House

Grace Alive Series

Christian Romance

- Grace Alive
- Grace Unbroken

Rebirth of the Prophesy Series

Sci-fi Romance

- Fatal Alien Affection

- Fatal Alien Attraction

The Jade Series

Epic Fantasy

- The Vullens' Curse
- The Deities' Touch
- The Vision Stone

Super Hero Princess Series

Middle grade/Young Adult

- Zara

Non-Fiction

- How to KEEP Writing Your Book
- Illustrated Sermons for Youth or Adults
- Grace Speaks

Printed in Great Britain
by Amazon